Read-About® Geography

Puerto Rico

By Elizabeth Zapata

Subject Consultant
Elvin E. Delgado
Doctoral Student
Department of Geography
Syracuse University
Syracuse, New York

Reading Consultant
Cecilia Minden-Cupp, PhD
Former Director of the Language and Literacy Program
Harvard Graduate School of Education
Cambridge, Massachusetts

Children's Press®
A Division of Scholastic Inc.
New York   Toronto   London   Auckland   Sydney
Mexico City   New Delhi   Hong Kong
Danbury, Connecticut

Designer: Herman Adler Design
Photo Researcher: Caroline Anderson
The photo on the cover shows a lighthouse along the coast in Punta Higuero,
Puerto Rico.

Library of Congress Cataloging-in-Publication Data

Zapata, Elizabeth, 1973–
  Puerto Rico / by Elizabeth Zapata.
      p. cm. — (Rookie read-about geography)
  Includes index.
  ISBN-10: 0-516-25387-5 (lib. bdg.)   0-531-16786-0 (pbk.)
  ISBN-13: 978-0-516-25387-9 (lib. bdg.)   978-0-531-16786-1 (pbk.)
    1. Puerto Rico—Juvenile literature. 2. Puerto Rico—Geography—Juvenile
literature. I. Title. II. Series.
  F1958.3.Z37 2006
  972.95—dc22   2005034957

CHILDREN'S PRESS, and ROOKIE READ-ABOUT®,
and associated logos are trademarks and/or registered trademarks
of Scholastic Library Publishing. SCHOLASTIC and associated logos
are trademarks and/or registered trademarks of Scholastic Inc.

1 2 3 4 5 6 7 8 9 10 R 16 15 14 13 12 11 10 09 08 07   08

Where can you find
millions of little frogs like
this one? Many tree frogs
live in Puerto Rico!

Puerto Rico is a commonwealth of the United States. This means that Puerto Rico has its own government but is still part of the United States.

Puerto Rico is an island to the southeast of Florida. Can you find Puerto Rico on this map?

CANADA

WASHINGTON

OREGON

IDAHO

MONTANA

NORTH DAKOTA

SOUTH DAKOTA

MINNESOTA

WISCONSIN

MICHIGAN

NEW HAMPSHIRE

VERMONT

MAINE

WYOMING

NEVADA

UTAH

COLORADO

NEBRASKA

IOWA

ILLINOIS

INDIANA

OHIO

PENNSYLVANIA

NEW YORK

MASSACHUSETTS

RHODE ISLAND

CONNECTICUT

NEW JERSEY

CALIFORNIA

ARIZONA

NEW MEXICO

KANSAS

OKLAHOMA

MISSOURI

ARKANSAS

KENTUCKY

TENNESSEE

WEST VIRGINIA

VIRGINIA

NORTH CAROLINA

DELAWARE

MARYLAND

Washington, D.C.

TEXAS

LOUISIANA

MISSISSIPPI

ALABAMA

GEORGIA

SOUTH CAROLINA

FLORIDA

North

West   East

South

MEXICO

ALASKA

CANADA

HAWAII

PUERTO RICO

There are many mountains
and hills in Puerto Rico.

Puerto Rico also has miles of sandy beaches. People like swimming in the clear, blue water.

Visitors to Puerto Rico enjoy exploring Río Camuy (REE-oh kah-MOO-ee) Cave Park.

This park features amazing caves and a river that flows underground!

A small waterfall in the Caribbean National Forest

Puerto Rico also has many rain forests. These forests receive much rainfall and are warm and tropical.

The Caribbean National Forest is a rain forest in Puerto Rico. It is home to more than 240 kinds of trees!

Puerto Rico's national tree is the silk-cotton tree. The silk-cotton tree can grow to be more than 150 feet (50 meters) tall!

The national flower is
the Puerto Rican hibiscus
(hi-BIS-kuhss).

Puerto Rico is home to many different animals. Some animals such as the Puerto Rican parrot can't be found anywhere else in the world.

Lizards, snakes, hawks, and bats all live in Puerto Rico.

Puerto Rico's national bird is the stripe-headed tanager (TA-ni-juhr).

Many people think of the tree frog as a symbol of Puerto Rico. A symbol is an object that stands for something else.

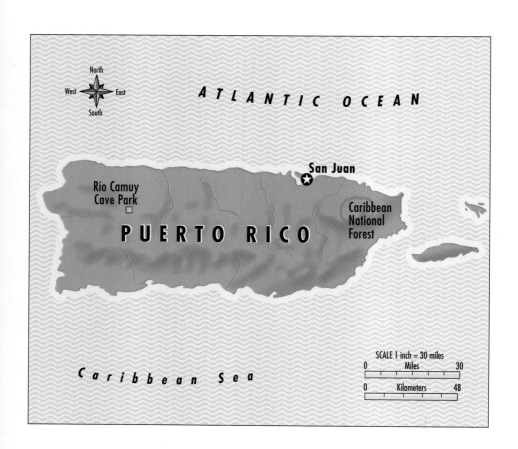

North
West · East
South

A T L A N T I C   O C E A N

San Juan

Río Camuy
Cave Park

PUERTO RICO

Caribbean
National
Forest

C a r i b b e a n   S e a

SCALE 1 inch = 30 miles
0   Miles   30
0   Kilometers   48

San Juan is the capital of Puerto Rico. It is also Puerto Rico's largest city.

More than 3 million people live in Puerto Rico. Many of them speak both Spanish and English.

Baseball is a popular sport in Puerto Rico.

Roberto Clemente (1934–1972) was a famous baseball player with the Pittsburgh Pirates. He was born in Puerto Rico.

21

Some farmers in Puerto Rico grow coffee or plantains (PLAN-taynz). Plantains are similar to bananas.

Plantains

Puerto Rican sugarcane plants

Other farmers grow a type of grass called sugarcane. Sugarcane plants are a source of sugar.

Puerto Rico has many factories. Some factories make medicine. Other factories turn sugarcane into sugar.

A worker makes medicine in a Puerto Rican factory.

Fried plantains

Puerto Rican meals almost always include rice.

Fried plantains also make a tasty treat!

There's plenty to do in Puerto Rico!

What will you do first when you visit?

Words You Know

Caribbean National Forest

plantains

Puerto Rican hibiscus

Río Camuy Cave Park

30

Roberto Clemente

silk-cotton tree

sugarcane

tree frog

31

Index

About the Author

Elizabeth Zapata is a second-generation Puerto Rican. Like many of her ancestors and family, she has settled in the Bronx, New York, but visits Puerto Rico at least twice a year. She wishes to instill in her daughter, Zoë, a love of this beautiful island.

Photo Credits

Photographs © 2007: Corbis Images: 25 (Bob Krist), 26 (PhotoCuisine); Danita Delimont Stock Photography/Michele Molinari: 9, 30 bottom right; Getty Images: 13, 30 bottom left (Andre Cezar), 22, 30 top right (Bruce James), 10, 30 top left (Mark Lewis/The Image Bank), 21, 31 top left (Photo File/Hulton Archive); ImageState/Medioimages: 7; Kevin Schafer: 14; Michael Danzenbaker: 17; Omni-Photo Communications/Chie Nishio: 29; Photo Researchers, NY: 15 (E.R. Degginger), 3, 31 bottom right (Dante Fenolio); Robert Fried Photography: cover, 6; Visuals Unlimited: 12, 31 top right (Norris Blake), 23, 31 bottom left (Inga Spence).

Maps by Bob Italiano